MORE RIDDLES, RIDDLES, RIDDLES

MORE RIDDLES, RIDDLES, RIDDLES

Selected by

HELEN HOKE

Pictures by

HARO

FRANKLIN WATTS/NEW YORK/LONDON/1976

Library of Congress Cataloging in Publication Data

Main entry under title:

More riddles, riddles, riddles.

   SUMMARY: Collections of riddles compiled un-
der chapter headings from "Atrocious" to "Zealous".
      1. Riddles—Juvenile literature. [1. Riddles]
I. Hoke, Helen, 1903–   II. Haro. III. Title.
PN6371.5.M6   1976   398.6   76–10696
ISBN 0–531–00351–5

Contents

atrocious!

●

What are the three quickest ways of sending a message?

Telephone, telegraph and tell a woman.

●

What is it that lives in winter, dies in summer, and grows with its roots upwards?

An icicle.

●

What do banks and trees have in common?

Branches everywhere.

●

What do we have on New Year's Day that we don't have any other day of the year?

A New Year, of course.

●

On what day of the year do children talk the least?

On the shortest day.

●

If life gets really tough, what have you that you can always count on?

Your fingers.

●

What must one do to have soft hands?

Nothing.

●

If a woman changed her sex, what religion would she be?

She would be a he-then (heathen).

●

What word of only three syllables combines in it absolutely all of twenty-six letters?

Alphabet.

●

What letter is the person you speak to?

U (you).

POOR: What things increase the more you contract them?
POORER: Debts.

•

DOPEY: On which side of a cup is the handle?
DOPIER: On the outside, of course, silly!

•

MAY: Why are washerwomen foolish?
JAY: Well, *imagine*—they set tubs to catch soft water when it rains hard!

•

SAGE: Why is life the biggest riddle of all riddles?
SEER: Because we must all give it up eventually.

•

Why is a window in the roof like the sun?
Because it's a skylight.

•

What is most like a horse's foot?
A mare's.

•

DOPEY: How do you spell Mississippi?
DOPIER: The river? Or the state?

•

Who is the most shining example of a luminary you have heard of?
The man in the moon.

FANNY: I don't Bolivia.
DANNY: Denmark my words, you'll regret it.

What age is the escape of fluid?
Leakage.

What made the poor manager so hard-boiled?
He'd been in hot water so many times.

What is a buttress?
A female butler.

What is a successful lawsuit?
The one worn by a policeman.

Why is tennis often an affectionate game?
Because the score usually contains love.

What is the best material for a barber's suit?
Haircloth.

Why did the amateur photographer take the worst possible, most pessimistic view of everything?
He was a candid camera fiend.

8

KING ARTHUR: How much'll you take for this armour, Lance?

SIR LANCELOT: Ten pence an ounce. You see, that's first-class mail.

●

WISE WINNIE says she would rather fool with a bee than be with a fool.

●

What should the sign say on a door for men only?
Gentrance.

●

Why did the loaf feel homesick for the oven?
Because that's where it was bred.

●

Why was Solomon's 999th wife nervous that her husband did not truly love her?
Because she was just one in a thousand.

●

Why is a forger a very moral person?
Because he is always ready to write a wrong.

●

What is Kleenex?
Everyone's daily nose-paper.

●

If she's narrow in her views—
Amplifier.

●

What animal would be most likely to devour a near-relation?
An ant-eater.

●

What is denial?
Where Cleopatra lived.

●

How was the man connected with the police station?
By a pair of handcuffs.

●

What is an inaccurate appraisal?
A guesstimate.

●

ITCHY: Doctor, did you say eating radishes would make my skin break out?
DOCTOR: No. I never make rash promises.

●

Why did they hang a certain picture?
Because they couldn't find the artist.

10

•

What are the constituents of quartz?

Pints.

•

What are the most suitable fabrics for a banker's clothing?

Checks, or cashmere.

•

Why is a pretty girl's face her fortune?

It draws a lot of interest.

•

EDUCATED EDDIE: I love to browse in a library.
DUMB DORA: High browse or low browse?

•

What is the difference between a lift and the man who runs it?

One is lowered to take passengers up, the other is hired to do it.

•

Which is the strongest day of the seven?

Sunday, because the others are week days.

•

CUSTOMER: Is the milk from this dairy pasteurized?
WAITRESS: It sure is. Every morning they turn their cows out to pasture.

•

What is the most musical grandfather a child could have?

One who fiddles with his beard.

•

When do ladies carry fire?

When they have taper-ed fingers.

•

What is hard to beat?

A hard-boiled egg.

•

How many hairs are there in a dog's tail?

None. They are all outside.

•

What are the most disagreeable articles for a man to keep on hand?

Hand-cuffs.

•

What is the name of the feathers that grow on the under-side of a chicken's wing?

Chicken feathers.

•

SMART: What is the difference between a primping girl and a soldier?
ALECK: The girl powders her face and the soldier faces powder.

•

TILLY: Why is a proud woman like a music book?
LILLY: She is full of airs.

•

HOOTER: Why is a gun like a jury?
SHOOTER: It goes off when discharged.

Why is an irritable man like a hard-baked loaf?

Because he is crusty.

bodacious!

•

If you asked a Doctor of Divinity to play on the violin, what term of contempt would you use?

Fiddle, D.D.!

•

What name besides Anna reads the same backwards and forwards?

Hannah.

•

SUE: Would it ever be pleasant to receive a blow?
PRUE: Well, maybe—if someone strikes you agreeably.

•

What pine has the sharpest needles?

The porcupine.

•

How old would you be if you were very, very fat?

The same age as you are now.

What is the pal of a happening?

Incident-ally.

Which animal is an automobile fond of?

Carpet.

What musical instrument is a nagger?

A harp.

What sounds wooden and weighty and yet is tiny?

Plankton.

What part of the body is especially right for Christmas?

Mistletoe.

What musical instrument is especially at home in the kitchen?

A kettledrum.

What American Indian weapon grows underground?

Arrowroot.

●

What shoe can speak—(but only with an accent?)
A brogue.

●

What are the strongest shellfish?
Mussels.

●

Where do little ears of corn come from?
The stalk brings them.

●

Who always whistles while he works?
A traffic policeman.

●

What's the difference between a hill and a pill?
A hill is hard to get up and a pill is hard to get down.

●

What is a volcano?
A mountain with hiccups.

●

What is a mayor?
A she-horse.

●

What did the mother ghost say to the baby ghost?
"Don't spook until spooken to."

•

What is as big as a dinosaur and doesn't weigh an ounce?

A dinosaur's shadow.

•

How can you tell that clocks are shy?

Because they always have their hands in front of their faces.

•

What is purple and goes "pooh-pooh"?

A purple pooh-pooh.

•

Why is an operation funny?

It leaves the patient in stitches.

•

Why was the Mama Owl worried about Baby?

Because he didn't give a hoot about anything.

•

How do you avoid that run-down feeling?

Look both ways before crossing the street.

•

Why aren't there any witches this year?

They're all on strike for electric brooms.

•

How do you grow hair on a billiard ball?

Who wants hair on a billiard ball!

•

What wears covering in the summer and goes bare in the winter?

A tree.

•

What works when it plays, and plays when it works?

A fountain.

•

PECK: Why is it hard to get a game of cricket started?
SNIFF: Because all bats like to sleep in the daytime, silly!

•

How can you tell that a ship is in love?

When she is attached to a buoy.

•

Why did the kitchen sink?

Because it saw the tap dance.

•

Why did the man take a bale of hay to bed?

To feed his nightmare.

What is the difference between a tube and a foolish Dutchman?

One is a hollow cylinder and the other a silly Hollander.

When is a ship at sea not on water?

When she is on fire.

Why don't women ever become bald as soon as men?
They wear their hair longer, of course.

What did arthritis say to rheumatism?
Let's get out of this joint.

EDUCATED EDDIE: What is it that can speak any language in the world?
SMART KID: An echo—what else?

Why do your nose and chin disagree?
Because so many words pass between them.

What man always finds things dull everywhere?
A knife-sharpener.

TEACHER: Georgie, what is a synonym?
LAZY GEORGIE: A synonym is a word you use when you can't spell the other one.

What parts of Nevada are in France?
The letters "N," "E," and "V."

What letter means just *one* of anything?
A.

●

Why is it economical to keep chickens?

Because for every grain they give a peck.

●

Why is T the most powerful letter?

It can even make a star start.

●

SYMPATHETIC SYBIL: Did the doctor treat you yesterday?

SICK ZACK: I should say not! He charged me fifteen pounds!

●

When should a baker stop baking doughnuts?

When he gets tired of the whole business.

●

POLLY: Have you ever heard a star speak?

MOLLY: Of course!—a movie star.

●

What letter belongs here: I am; we . . . ?

R (are).

●

What are the two strangest happenings you ever heard of?

About when a deaf and dumb man picked up a wheel and spoke, and a blind man picked up a hammer and saw.

22

What is the best butter in the world?

The goat.

SMART: If you had a box of candles, but no matches, how would you light them?
SMARTER: Easy: simply take one candle out of the box, then the box would be a candle-lighter.

What is there about a house that seldom falls, but never really hurts the tenant when it does?

The rent.

Why did Joseph's brethren put him in the pit?

Because they thought it a nice opening for a young man.

•

Why does a chestnut horse never pay toll?
Because his master pays it.

•

MARTY: How many balls of cord would it take to reach the moon?
SMARTY: Only one, if it was long enough.

•

When is a spotted dog most likely to enter the house?
When the door is open.

Capricious!

●

WILLY: When is coffee like the soil?
NILLY: When it is ground.

●

Why do you always put on your left shoe last?
When you have put on one, the other is left.

●

Why are many unlucky people like umbrellas?
They have so many ups and downs.

●

If you had a farm, how could you get eggs without keeping hens?
Keep ostriches.

●

What is that animal which has the head of a cat, and the tail of a cat, and the ways of a cat, and yet which isn't a cat?
A kitten.

• Which is the rudest bird?

The mocking bird, of course.

• Why is a dirty child like flannel?

Because it shrinks from washing.

• When is a nation like a baby?

When it is in arms.

• Why is a brand-new baby like a gale of wind?

Because it begins with a squall.

• Why did the match box?

Because it saw the wood fence.

●

How can you be sure the engine of your car isn't missing?

Look inside.

●

ROBIN: What is the least dangerous kind of robbery?
ROBBER: Safe robbery!

●

What is the difference between a tailor and a stable-boy?

One mends a tear, the other tends a mare.

●

What is the difference between a hat and a baby?

The one you wear, the other you were.

●

CUSTOMER, *in a newspaper office:* I would like to have copies of your paper for a week back.
CLERK: Why don't you try a plaster cast?

●

Why is a watch dog bigger by night than by day?

Because he is let out at night and taken in by day.

●

What is that which divides by uniting, and unites by dividing?

Scissors.

Why are playing cards like wolves?
Because they come in a pack.

GOOFY: How come Little Bo Peep lost her sheep?
GOOFIER: No wonder! She had a crook with her!

MANDY: Why is a lovely young lady like a hinge?
SANDY: Oh—well—she is something to adore!

Who introduced walking sticks?

Eve, when she presented Adam with a little Cain (cane).

Why is a good resolution like a fainting lady?
Because it certainly ought to be carried out.

SMART: What does an envelope feel like when it is licked?
ALECK: No one knows. It just shuts up and says nothing about it!

When rain falls, does it ever get up again?
Oh, yes—in dew time.

When is an attic like a grove of trees?
When it is full of trunks.

What is the difference between a railway guard and a school master?
One minds the train, the other trains the mind.

Why is "A" like high noon?
Because it comes in the middle of day.

DOPEY: What time is it?

SMARTY: Five o'clock.

DOPEY, *wonderingly*: Well, how do you like *that?* I've been asking people all day long what time it is, and everybody tells me something different every time.

•

Why does a bald-headed man have no use for keys?

Because he has lost his locks.

•

DUMB SAILOR: Why is distance by sea not measured by miles, as it is on land?

CRANKY CAPTAIN: Just because it is knot!

•

What can go over the water and through the water without ever getting wet?

Sunlight and moonbeams.

•

What is better than presence of mind in a train wreck?

Absence of body, of course.

•

How can you spell "enemy" in three letters?

NME is one way: FOE's another way.

What animals took least luggage into the Ark?

The fox and cock, who had only a brush and comb between them.

What letter asks a question?

Y (why).

TEACHER: Which carpenter's tool can you spell forward and backward the same way?
SMART BOY: Level.

•

Why was the enemy alien rounded up for trial?
He had arms up his sleeves.

•

What game might give you a chill?
Draughts.

•

What is the difference between a cloud and a boy being spanked?
The cloud pours with rain and the boy roars with pain.

•

What is the best thing to put into pies?
Your teeth.

•

What insect does a blacksmith manufacture?
He makes the firefly.

•

MOTHER: What do you want to take your cod liver oil with this morning, Timmy?
TIMMY: A fork.

•

What did the beaver say to the tree?
It's been nice gnawing you.

32

●

Why do ships have round portholes?

So the seawater won't hit the passengers square in the eye.

●

DORIS: Did you ever hear the story about the two holes in the ground?
BORIS: Well, well!

●

What happens to geese when they fly upside-down?
They quack up!

●

What makes opening a piano so difficult?
The keys are on the inside.

●

Why are flowers lazy?
Well, they're usually in their beds.

●

What kind of a bow is impossible to tie?
A rainbow.

●

Why do you do your arithmetic lessons with a pencil?
Because the pencil can't do them without you.

●

What do bees do to earn a living?
They cell their honey.

33

•

Why is a duck like an icicle?
Because they both grow down.

•

What can you swallow that can also swallow you?
Water.

•

Why did the sunbeam?
Maybe because it saw the skylark?

•

What is a serenade of cats in the night called?
Meowsic.

•

On what kind of a ride were the gunmen taking the man?
A slay ride, of course.

•

Why is a cat's tail like the end of the world?
'Cause it's so fur to the end.

•

TEACHER: An anecdote is a tale. Now, how can you use it in a sentence?
STUDENT: I tied a tin can to the dog's anecdote.

•

What is slush?
Who cares?—it's snow matter.

34

•

Why did the drummer think he would make a good policeman?

Because he was used to pounding a beat.

•

CONCEITED CLAUDE: What is the difference between a bird with one wing and a bird with two wings?
DOPEY DAN: I give it up.
CONCEITED CLAUDE: A difference of a pinion.

•

Why did the boy stop going to barber college?

He was a shear leader . . . then they threw him out for cutting a class.

•

What is a painless dentist?

One with a broken window.

•

If her hands are cold—

Heater.

•

CURIOUS CARL wants to know why a pantomimist cannot tickle nine Esquimaux.
WISE WILFRED replies it's because he can gesticulate.

•

What did the ground say to the rain?

"My name's mud now!"

●

Why is the letter K like a pig's tail?

Because it is at the end of pork.

●

What would you call a man who is always wiring for money?

An electrician.

●

Why is a baker like a beggar?

He kneads bread.

●

Why did the burglar cut the legs off his bed?

So he could lay low for a while.

●

SMART: Why can't a cook swallow his apron?
ALECK: Because it goes against his stomach.

delirious!

If your neighbour quarrelled with you and called you some kind of insect, would he be wrong?

Yes, an insect has six legs.

Is kleptomania catching?

No, it's taking.

Why would you take a ruler to bed with you at night?

To find out how long you slept.

KIM: Why should a boy named Ben marry a girl called Anne?

TIM: Because she would be Benny-fitted, and he would be Annie-mated.

●   ●

Why doesn't the clock strike 14?
It hasn't the face to do it.

●

Why is the horse the most humane of all animals?
Because, for one thing, he listens to every woe.

●

What are all the little rivers and streams that run into the Nile?
Juve-niles.

●

How far is it around the world?
Only a day—for the sun!

●

What nut has a hole in the middle?
A doughnut.

●

What did Adam do when he wanted sugar?
Raised Cain.

●

LAWYER: What suits last much longer than people want them to?
TAILOR: Lawsuits.

●

When does a dog look like a boy?
Whenever he takes after one.

When a shoemaker is about to make a shoe, what is the first thing he uses?

The last, of course.

SUSPICIOUS SUE: Why can't you ever trust a bee?
SOUR SAL: Because the darned thing's a humbug!

Why is a very old car like a very young baby?

Because it never goes anywhere without a rattle.

If you bit off a fellow's nose and he sued you about it, what would the judge admonish you to do?

To keep the piece (peace).

What is the age of communication?
Postage.

●

What is that which has never been felt, seen nor heard, never existed and still has a name?
Nothing.

●

SMUG: What is the right way to finish a letter?
SMUGGER: Write it!

What happens when a light falls into the water at an angle of ninety degrees?
It goes out at any angle.

●

HIGH SCHOOL BOY *(to clerk)*: I'd like a box of pencils, please.
CLERK: Hard or soft?
HIGH SCHOOL BOY: Extra soft. They're for writing love letters.

●

What ten-letter word starts with "petrol?"
Automobile.

●

SANDY: Why did the famous cricketer make so much money?
ANDY: Ho! Anyone knows a good batter makes good dough!

What is the difference between a pretty girl and a mouse?

One charms the he's, the other harms the cheese.

What is the difference between a cat and a comma?

The cat has claws at the end of his paws: the comma is a pause at the end of a clause.

extemporaneous!

●

What is always filled when in use and empty when at rest?

A shoe.

●

Why are chickens such big eaters?

Because they take a peck at a time.

●

What is the craziest bird?

A loon.

●

HAPPY: When does a man wear a large watch?
GO-LUCKY: When he wants to have a big time, I imagine.

●

What do all ships weigh, no matter what size they are?

Anchors.

●

Why did the moron cut his fingers off?

Because he wanted to write shorthand.

SILLY: Why is it bad to write on an empty stomach?
BILLY: Oh, it isn't so bad—but paper is better.

•

Who was Jonah's teacher?
The whale who brought him up.

•

What letter means yourself?
I.

•

BESSIE: Honey, which letters *make* honey?
BEANY: The B's, Bessie.

•

When is water like a kangaroo?
When it makes a spring.

•

Why is a jailer like a pianist?
Because he fingers the keys.

•

LOVELORN: Why do girls kiss each other, but men do not?
BOY: Because girls have nothing better to kiss—and men have!

44

Why did the city rat gnaw a hole in the carpet?
He wanted to see the floor show.

Why is winter the best time to buy thermometers?
Because in summer, they are higher.

What ant lives in a house?
An occupant.

●

Why should a horse not be hungry on a journey?

Because he always has a bit in his mouth.

●

What usually loses its head by day but gets it back at night?

A pillow.

●

Which is the easier to spell—fiddle-de-dee or fiddle-de-dum?

The former, of course, because it is spelled with more e's (ease).

fatuous!

●

Why is it bad to look at Niagara Falls too long?
You might get a cataract in your eye.

●

Little Boy: Which is the best land for very young children?
Mother: Lapland, surely.

●

What is the ugliest hood one can have?
A falsehood.

●

Why will the first clock on the moon be called something crazy?
Because it will have a luna(r) tick.

●

When is an eye not an eye?
When an onion makes it water.

●

Sue: When is a spanking like a hat?
Prue: When it is felt.

47

●

Who was the best business woman in the Bible?

Pharoah's daughter. She drew a profit (prophet) from a rush on the bank.

●

When is it correct to serve milk in a saucer?

When you feed the cat.

●

Why is a crow a brave bird?

Easy. He never shows a white feather.

●

What is the best way to hide a bear?

Skin him.

●

Why is a baby boy always welcome?

Because he never comes amiss.

SUNDAY-SCHOOL TEACHER: Who was older, David or Goliath?
VAGUE VERA: Well, David *must* have been, because the Bible says he rocked Goliath to sleep.

What is the difference between a man going upstairs and one looking up?

One is stepping up stairs and the other is staring up steps.

What is the difference between a lover and a rejected suitor?

One kisses the miss, and the other misses the kiss.

What's the good of having a whole paper of pins?

It will give you many good points.

Who are the best bookkeepers?

People who never return the books you lend them.

What would the spider have done if he had found himself late and alone in going into the Ark?

Taken a fly.

49

How can you shoot a thousand hares at one shot?

Fire at a wig.

grievous!

•

STUDENT: Is there a word in the English language that contains all the vowels?
TEACHER, *with alacrity:* Unquestionably!

•

Which travels faster, heat or cold?
Heat, of course. You can *catch* cold.

•

NEW CAR-BUYER: What is the difference between 1971 and 1975 model cars?
OLD CAR-DRIVER: Four years—and a lot of depreciation!

•

How can you keep postage stamps from sticking together?
Buy one at a time.

•

What will soon be yesterday and was tomorrow?
Today.

MAY: Why is a kiss like gossip?
JAY: Because it goes from mouth to mouth.

•

Why would an Italian barber rather shave six
Italians than one Tunisian?
Because he would get six times as much money.

•

Why does a policeman wear metal buttons on his
coat?
So he can button it up.

•

Why is a thief very comfortable?
Because he takes things easy.

•

OLDER BROTHER: Which burn longer, the candles
on a boy's birthday cake, or on a man's birthday
cake?
SMART BABY BROTHER: They *all* burn shorter, silly!

heinous!

●

What can you still keep on having, even after you have given it away?

A cold.

●

What gets wetter the more it dries?

A towel.

●

What is that which can play actively, yet can't even walk?

A piano.

FLO: What is a rabbit called who has never been outside the house?
JOE: An ingrown hare.

•

SMARTY: Why were the elephants the last animals to leave the Ark?
ARTY: They had to pack their trunks.

•

SHINY: What makes people bald-headed?
PATE: Lack of hair—what else?

54

•

What is musically dangerous about an icy street?

You must C-sharp or you'll B-flat.

•

LITTLE GIRL: Why does lightning shock people?
PRIM AUNTIE: Because it doesn't know how to conduct itself!

•

What leads fashion, yet is always out of date?

The letter F.

•

What has nothing left but a nose when it loses an eye?

Noise.

•

If you go shopping for twenty-five pence worth of long, thin tacks, what do you want them for?

Twenty pence, of course.

•

PREACHER: When is it right for you to lie?
LITTLE PAUL: When you are in bed.

•

Which is better, an old ten-pound note or a new one?

An old ten rather than a new one.

•

What horse lives underground?
A horseradish.

•

LEO: What usually happens when there is a big flood?
CLEO: Ooh! A river just all of a sudden gets too big for its bridges!

•

Why are a gun and the earth frighteningly alike?
They are both revolvers.

•

Why is the sun like a well-made loaf of bread?
Because it's light when it rises.

•

What's always divine?
What grapes grow on.

•

What is always broken before it is of any use?
An egg.

•

Why is a lollipop like a horse?
Because the more you lick it, the faster it goes.

56

How do you keep from being thirsty at night?

Sleep on a mattress with springs in it.

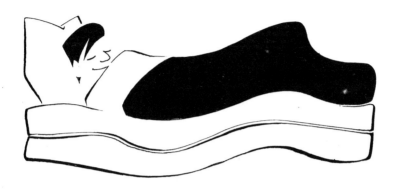

What kind of dog has no tail?

A hot dog.

DOPEY DAN: What did one tonsil say to the other?
CLEVER CARL: "It's Spring again, here comes a swallow."

Fashions change, but what can a person wear that is never out of style?

A smile.

What have you that is most useful when it is used up?

An umbrella.

Why did Johnny's mother knit him three stockings when he was so long away in the army?

Because Johnny wrote her that he had got so tall he had grown another foot!

What most resembles a hen stealin'?

A cock robin.

Why do you suppose that a train never sits down?

Because it has a tender behind.

Why is a man who is always complaining the easiest man to satisfy?

Because nothing satisfies him.

HUNTER: Would it annoy a sparrow to call him a quail?
BUNTER: Naturally! You would be making game of him!

When is a baby not a baby?

When it's a little cross.

What do liars do after death?

Lie still.

WISE: Why is a man who never bets as bad as a gambler?
GUY: Because he is no better!

What is the difference between a prize fighter and a man with a cold?

One knows his blows, the other blows his nose.

SMUG: Why is a poor friend better than a rich one?
SMUGGER: Because a friend in need is a friend indeed.

What has probably happened when a cat goes into a cellar with four feet and comes out with eight?

It has maybe caught a mouse.

Why do little ducks go to the bank of the river?

To liquidate their little bills.

What is the correct height for people to stand?

At least over two feet.

impious!

●

If George's father is Tom's son, what kin is Tom to George?

George's grandfather.

●

TEACHER: Why are books your best friends?
WISE WILLY: Because, if they bore you, you can shut them up without making them angry.

●

What is the difference between 16 ounces of lead and a pianist?

The lead weighs a pound, and the pianist pounds away.

●

Why is a bubble like a bruise?

Because it also comes from a blow.

●

SMARTY: Who ever was born but never died?
PANTS: You—and millions of others.

●

Why is a big snowstorm a very popular joke?

Because everybody can see the drift.

●

What is the difference between a sewing machine and a kiss?

One sews nice, the other seems so nice.

●

NATURALIST: Why should we all pity poor turtles?
REALIST: Because theirs is such a hard case, we really should shell out for them!

●

Why is snow like an apple tree?

Because it leaves in the spring.

●

What makes a pig medically the most unusual animal in the world?

Because you first kill him, then you cure him.

●

PROFESSOR: Why should the number two hundred and eighty-eight never be mentioned in company?
FASTIDIOUS FRANCES: Because it is just *too* gross!

●

What letter is a printer's measure?

M (em).

62

•

Why are balloons like beggars?

Because they have no visible means of support.

•

MR. POOR: What's so unusual about money?
MR. RICH: Because you have to make it first before
you can make it last.

•

Why is a lazy clergyman like England?

He expects every man to do *his* duty.

•

What can a man give to a woman that he can't give to a man?

His name.

•

What horse can see as well behind as he does in front?

A blind horse.

•

Why are prairies so flat?

Because the sun sets on them every night.

•

Why should you always carry a watch when you cross a tropical desert?

Because there's a spring in it.

•

What nut is a large nation?

Brazil nut.

•

What is the best way to have a duck for dinner?

Go jump in the lake.

64

Why is a tree like a dog?

Because they both lose their bark when they die.

BREATHLESS BEN: What did the brave little mouse do when he came home and found his house on fire?
DRAMATIC DOLLY: He dived right in, dragged his children out, then gave them mouse-to-mouse resuscitation.

What sea creatures are the laziest?

Oysters, because they are *always* in their beds.

•

When does a man call his wife "honey?"
When she has a comb in her hair.

•

STEW: What kind of men are most apt to go to heaven?
PID: Dead men, silly!

•

What are the two most difficult surgical operations?
To take the jaw out of a woman and the cheek out of a man.

•

What are taxes?
Little nails.

etcetera, etcetera, etcetera!

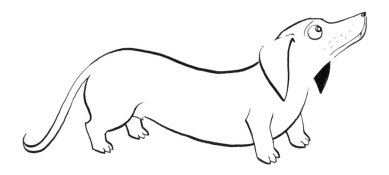

•

"Is she Hungary?" Bobby asked.

"Alaska," said Benny.

"Yes, Siam," she replied.

"All right. I'll Fiji," Bobby offered.

"Oh, don't Russia," Benny pleaded.

"What if she Wales?" Bobby demanded.

"Give her a Canada Chile," Benny suggested.

"I'd rather Turkey," she said, "except that I can't have any Greece."

When the waiter brought the bill, Benny urged Bobby, "I say, look and see how much has Egypt you."

•

There once was a man from Nantucket
Who kept all his cash in a bucket;
    But his daughter, named Nan,
    Ran away with a man,
And as for the bucket, Nantucket.
But he followed the pair to Pawtucket—
The man and the girl with the bucket;
    And he said to the man
    He was welcome to Nan,
But as for the bucket, Pawtucket.

•

The bottle of perfume that Willie sent
Was highly displeasing to Millicent;
    Her thanks were so cold
    They quarrelled, I'm told,
Through that silly scent Willie sent Millicent.

more etcetera!

●

Meet a few of the Sister States in the United States:
Mary Land, Ida Hoe and Minne Sota.

●

Conversation on a bus:
    "When did you find your husband?"
    "On Manday."
    "And when did he ask you to be his bride?"
    "On Chooseday."
    "When did you get married?"
    "On Wedsday."
    "And when the children came, when were they
      happiest?"
    "On Toysday."
    "But you finally had to consult a psychiatrist?"
    "On Freuday."
    "Because you were feeling low?"
    "On Sadderday."
    "And were avoiding everybody?"
    "On Shunday."

Business Reports:

"My business is looking up," said the astronomer.

"Mine is going up in smoke," complained the cigar maker.

"Mine is all right," chuckled the author.

"Mine is just sew, sew," remarked the tailor.

"Mine is growing," boasted the farmer.

"Mine is pretty light," snapped the electrician.

"Mine is picking up," smiled the cheerful potato picker.

"Mine is looking better," commented the optician.

laborious!

•

What colour is most easily heard?

A loud colour, of course.

•

NEWLY: What happens to a man who misses his train on his way home to a dinner party—his wife has everything ready to eat?
WED: He sure catches it after he gets home!

•

What are a person's last teeth called?

False.

•

What is the difference between a pretty baby girl and a nightgown.

One is born to wed, and the other is worn to bed.

•

When did Jacob sleep five in a bed?

When he slept with his fore-(four) fathers.

●

MOLLY: When was beef the highest that it has ever been?

JOLLY: That time the cow jumped over the moon.

●

What letter is an oriental man's pigtail?

·(ǝnǝnb) Ọ

●

SOLLY: Why is a looking-glass unlike a chattering girl?

PRECOCIOUS POLLY: The one reflects without speaking, the others speaks without reflecting.

●

ROMANTIC KAY: What was Adam's favourite popular song?

ROMANTIC RAY: "There's Only One Girl in This World for Me," of course.

●

What should a barber study?

All the short cuts.

●

Why are frogs such delicate animals?

Because they croak so easily.

●

What has hair outside and hair inside, yet people keep stuffing still more hair into it?

A fur cap.

●

What would happen if you crossed a chicken and a poodle?

The chicken would lay pooched eggs!

●

What city is for telegraph operators?

Electri-city.

●

What is that which Adam never had, yet gave two to each of his children?

Parents.

●

Why did the lady go outside with her purse open?

Because she expected some change in the weather.

SMART: Why did the little boy keep his bike near his bed?

SMARTER, *with a yawn:* Oh, he got tired of walking in his sleep.

●

What must you always do first, before getting off a bus?

Get on it.

●

WIMPY: Why is the telephone company not going to have telephone poles any longer?

IMPY: Hee! Hee! Because they are long enough now!

●

VISITOR: Why is a great bore like a tree?

TIRED HOST: Because both appear best when leaving.

●

What is the best way to grow fat?

Raise pigs.

●

Why should a man's hair turn grey before his moustache does?

Because it is older.

74

●

Why did the lawyer take a ladder to work?
So he could take his case to a higher court.

●

How can broken bones make themselves useful?
They can begin to knit.

•

Why is a room full of married folks like an empty room?

Easy: there is not a single person in it.

•

When are electricians most successful?

When they make good connections.

•

It never soars about the sky, yet often taken a fly; what is it?

A spider.

•

What is the difference between a boy who has fallen into a fire and a tortoise-shell cat?

One is a kindled brat, the other is a brindled cat.

•

What asks no questions but needs many answers?

A doorbell.

•

GANG: What did the picture say to the wall?
STER: First they framed me—then they hung me!

monstrous!

●

What is the difference between the earth and the sea?

One is dirt-y, the other tide-y.

●

What nation is the laziest nation?

Procrasti-nation.

●

How can you make a pearl out of a pear?

Add L to it.

●

What can you find to eat that nobody on earth ever saw before?

You can crack open a peanut and eat the kernel.

●

What runs around town all day and lies around all night, with its tongue hanging out?

Your shoe.

What was the largest island in the world before Australia was discovered?

Australia was always the largest.

How can you change a pumpkin into a squash?

Throw it up and it will come down a-squash.

Mrs. Rich: If you had an elegant country estate like mine, and owned a peacock—if it laid eggs in your neighbour's yard, who would *own* the eggs?
Poor Friend: Silly! Peacocks don't lay eggs.

Gang: What did the rug say to the floor?
Ster: Hands up! I've got you covered!

•

What kind of hen lays the longest?
A dead one.

•

What are nitrates?
Cheaper than day-rates.

•

What is the most modest piece of furniture?
The clock, because it always runs itself down.

•

What did Adam first plant in the garden of Eden?
His foot.

•

What is it that every boy and girl spend much time making, yet no one can ever see it when made?
Noise.

•

TEACHER: Every morning Farmer Brown had eggs for breakfast—but he didn't own any chickens, and he never got any eggs from chickens owned by anyone else. So where did he get the eggs?
STAR PUPIL: From his ducks.

•

What day of the year is a command to move on?
Easy! March 4th!

79

●

SMART: What has a thousand needles but does not sew?
SMARTER: A porcupine.

●

Why do you forget a tooth immediately after it's pulled out?
Because it goes right out of your head.

●

Why are every man's pants too short?
Because, no matter what, two feet of his legs stick out.

●

Why would it be better if needle were spelled with an "I"?
Because a needle is no good without an eye.

●

Which is the only way a leopard can change his spots?
By going from one spot to another.

●

What is a healthy job in winter?
Selling newspapers—for each copy sold increases circulation.

80

●

What is the difference between a well-dressed man and a tired dog?

The man wears a complete suit, the tired dog just pants.

●

What ant is the youngest?
An infant.

●

What is the difference between forms and ceremonies?
We sit on forms, but we stand on ceremonies.

●

What makes a light furious?
When it is put out.

●

What islands should have good singers?
The Canary Islands.

-

When could all of England have been bought for a really low amount?

When Richard the Third offered his kingdom for a horse.

-

Why is it easier for potatoes to grow better than other vegetables?

Because they have eyes to see what they are doing.

-

Why is a nutmeg like the window of a jail?

It has to be grated to be useful.

-

If a little dog should lose his tail, where could he get another?

At a retail store.

-

What cow has no courage?

A coward.

nauseous!

•

When does a man become chicken-hearted?
When he is henpecked.

•

What was the most plentiful fruit in the Ark?
Preserved pairs (pears).

•

Why is it easy to rob an old man's house?
Because his locks are apt to be few.

•

Though I dance at a ball, yet I am nothing at all.
What *am* I?
A shadow.

•

1ST CHARACTER: What is the difference between a crazy hare and a counterfeit bill?
2ND CHARACTER: One is a mad bunny, the other is bad money.

●

SMART: Which is correct to say, 6 plus 8 *is* 12, or
are 12?
SMARTER: Pooh! Neither: 6 plus 8 are 14.

●

How can you tell a jeweller from a jailor?
One sells watches, the other watches cells.

●

What is the best way to make a fire with two sticks?
Be very sure that one of them is a match!

●

What does everyone have that a bottle has, too?
A neck.

HUNGRY: Waiter! I'm in a hurry! Will the griddle cakes be long?
FELLOW: No, sir, round!

●

Which women live longer than men?
Widows.

●

What should you do if you woke up in the night, and heard a mouse squeaking?
Oil it, of course.

●

If you invited a toad to your party, what would you sit him on?
A toadstool?

●

TEACHER: What is wind?
SMARTY: Air in a hurry!

●

BARRY: Are you going to take the train home?
LARRY: No, my father would only make me take it back.

●

When are you closely related to a fish?
When your grandmother is a good old soul.

●

What age is to search thoroughly?
Rummage.

●

How do you greet mosquitoes?
Pat them on the back.

●

PATTY: Are you going to see your new boyfriend Samoa?
HATTY: Don't be Sicily, he's Spain in the neck.

●

Who lives off the fat of the land?
A girdle manufacturer.

What is a European bell?
Belgium.

What is the centre of gravity?
The letter V.

When is a man like a snake?
When he is rattled.

CLEVER CARL says that many men smoke but
Fu Manchu.

How might you be completely sleepless for seven
days and still not lack any rest?
By sleeping at night.

What is a patterned partner?
A checkmate.

Why is a clock like a man sentenced to death?
Its hours are numbered.

BILLY: Do you like cycling with a party?
SILLY: No, I prefer to cyclone.

●

What is alive and has only one foot?

A leg.

●

Smart: What did the cannibal army have for breakfast?
Aleck: Baked beings.

Outrageous!

●

FUN-PUN WORDS:
Watch out, Bean,
He's stringing you.

●

You tell 'em, Church Bell,
I tolled *you*.

●

You set it up, Printer,
I'm not your type.

●

Don't let them scare you, Shoemaker,
You know awl.

●

You tell 'em, Butcher,
You've got some tongue.

●

You tell 'em, Pie,
You've got the crust!

●

You tell 'em, Mountain,
I'm only a bluff.

●

You tell 'em, Submarine,
I can't seaplane.

●

You tell 'em, Calendar,
You've got lots of time.

●

You tell 'em, Horse,
You've got a tale.

●

You tell 'em, Cat,
That's what you're fur.

●

You tell 'em, Gambler,
You've got winning ways.

•

You tell 'em, Dictionary,
You're full of facts.

•

You tell 'em, Bald Head,
You're smooth.

•

You tell 'em, Cemetery,
You are so grave.

•

You tell 'em, Clock,
You've got the time.

•

You tell 'em, Electricity,
You can shock 'em.

•

You tell 'em, June,
And don't July.

•

You tell 'em, Skyscraper,
You have more than one storey.

poisonous!

What is taller sitting down than standing up?
A cat.

When may a man be said to be over head and ears in debt?
When he hasn't paid for his wig.

Why is a joke like a coconut?
Because it's no good until it is cracked.

Who combines extragavance and caution?
A spendthrift.

•

What kinds of servants are best for hotels?
The inn-experienced.

•

What kind of umbrella does a minister's wife carry
on a rainy day?
A wet one.

•

What is an electrical cat?
A cathode.

•

SILLY: I see in the papers that a guy ate six dozen
pancakes.
BILLY: Oh, how waffle!

•

What is a boy?
A noise with dirt on it, and a coat pocket containing
maybe a live frog, a penny, a piece of toffee, and
some foreign stamps.

•

Who was the strongest man in the Bible?
Jonah, because the whale couldn't keep him down.

•

EDGAR: Do you know Poe's Raven?
ALLAN: No, what's he mad about?

•

What is the boldest city in the world?
Audacity.

•

What is the difference between a very old woman and a cow?

One lives in the past, the other in the pasture.

•

What well-known game is an invisible colour?

Blind-man's buff.

•

What is a medical bell?

Belladonna.

•

Who killed one-fourth of all the people in the world?

Cain, when he killed Abel.

•

What has lots of heads but can't think?

A box of matches.

•

Why are seeds when sown like gateposts?

Because they propagate.

•

What cat is best suited to a violinist?

Catgut.

•

What is a war-like bell?

Belligerent.

●

What fish has its eyes closest together?
The smallest fish.

●

What was the camel's favourite saying?
"I have a hunch!"

●

If cheese comes after dinner, what comes after cheese?
Mice.

●

What is the best material for an editor to wear?
Prints.

What's the difference between a high mountain and a spoonful of epsom salts?

One's hard to get up, the other is hard to get down.

•

What jewel is found on another planet?

A moonstone.

•

Who was the fastest runner in the Bible?

Adam, because he was first in the human race.

•

What has four legs and feathers?

A featherbed.

•

ENGAGED GIRL: You got cheated on this diamond ring.
BEAU: I don't think so. I know my onions.
ENGAGED GIRL: Maybe—but not your carats.

•

Why is snow different from Sunday?

Because it can fall on any day of the week.

•

If you were to plant a puppy, what kind of tree would come up?

A dogwood.

●

What is the difference between a ballet dancer and a duck?

One goes quick on her legs; the other goes quack on her eggs.

●

POLLY: I hear that your fiancé is doing settlement work.

MOLLY: Yes, his creditors finally caught up with him.

•

What is one Irish bell?

Belfast.

•

Why is a mouse like hay?

Because the cat'll eat it.

•

What age is to soothe or relieve?

Assuage.

•

What nasty thing did the new suitcase say to the old, beat-up one?

"You're a sad case!"

•

What animal doesn't play fair?

The cheetah.

•

What part of a tree is necessary to a book?

A leaf.

querulous!

●

MATTY: Why should a greedy man wear a plaid shirt?
FATTY: To keep a check on his stomach, of course.

●

What ship has no soft berths?
Hardship.

●

How can you tell that the rooster is very fussy about his possessions?
Because he won't lend anyone his comb.

●

What is it of which the common kind is best?

Sense.

●

Why is death like someone breaking your windows?

Because it puts an end to your panes.

●

Why are fishermen and shepherds not to be trusted?

Because they all live by hook and by crook.

●

Why is the chef to the President of France like a bin of coal?

Because he feeds the great (grate).

●

What is the best name for the wife of a gas man?

Meta.

●

What age is fodder for livestock?

Silage.

●

RAY: I'll stick to you like glue, my darling.
FAY: The feeling is mucilage, my love.

●

Why is it reasonable for carpenters to believe there is no such thing as stone?

Because they never saw it.

100

What is the difference between a photograph and a whole family with measles?

One is a fac-simile, and the other is a sick family.

What is a supernatural hobby?

Witchcraft.

What ability can be counted on?

Predictability.

•

What age is good to eat?
Sausage.

•

JEWELLER'S SON: Dad, how do you just a watch?
JEWELLER: Adjust, son—not just just.
JEWELLER'S SON: Well, Dad, if you add just to just, it's just just, isn't it?

•

What is the difference between a dog losing his hair, and a man painting a small building?
One sheds his coat, the other coats his shed.

•

CITY BOY: How many heifers have you got?
FARMER: Heifer dozen.

•

Why did the boy want to work in a bank?
He heard there was money in it.

•

Why does everybody else have more money in his pocket than you have?
Because you never have *any* money in *his* pocket.

•

What ability is steady?
Stability.

102

ridiculous!

●

What kin is preserved?
Gherkin.

●

How do we know that mosquitoes are happy?
They always sing at their work.

●

What is the age of cultivating land?
Tillage.

●

If you woke up on a dark night on a camping trip,
what would you do for a light?
Take a feather from the pillow; that's light enough.

●

What is the keynote of good manners?
B-natural.

●

When is coffee like the soil?
When it is ground.

What fur did Adam and Eve wear?
Bare-skin.

What did Lot's wife turn to before she turned to salt?
She turned to rubber.

Why do women put their hair in rollers?
To wake up curly in the morning.

If your neighbour were to see you riding on a donkey, what fruit would you remind him of?
A pair.

BERNIE: How can I make anti-freeze?
ERNIE: Hide her woollen nightie.

What kind of news is the most orderly?
Information.

What is a church cat?
A cathedral.

ANGRY HUSBAND: I don't mean to Russia, but Venice that cook leaving?
WIFE: Well, she said yesterday she wasn't going to Rumania here another day.

•

What kin has awkward manners?
Bumpkin.

•

What is the hottest bird?
The firebird.

•

What can sometimes have more than a hundred feet?
A skating rink.

•

What age is good for tying things?
Cordage.

•

SANDY: Do you know Art?
ANDY: Art who?
SANDY: Artesian.
ANDY: Sure. I know Artesian well.

•

What was the family doing when the fuse blew?
Sitting in the dark.

●

What ability is good-natured?

Amiability.

●

What is the difference between a cat jumping and a match?

One lights on its feet, the other lights on its head.

●

CURIOUS CARL: Why do they call it a libel suit?
SHREWD SAM: Because you're liable to win and you're liable to lose.

●

What men are most aboveboard in their movements?

Chessmen.

●

What flowers do shepherds watch?

Phlox.

●

Why is a theatre such a sad place?

Because all the seats are in tiers.

●

If a man should smash a clock, would he be accused of killing time?

Not if the clock struck first.

106

●

Smart: Who was the earth's greatest thief?
Smarter: Atlas, because he held up the world.

●

What ship is always managed by more than one person?

Partnership.

●

When do you spell best?

When the teacher asks you to.

●

TERRY: I saw a big rat in my kitchen oven, and when I went for my revolver he ran out.
JERRY: Did you shoot him?
TERRY: No. He was out of my range.

●

What are always running along the streets in a town?
Curbs.

●

What sort of wind do we look for after Lent?
An Easter-ly one.

●

Why is a greedy man like one with a poor memory?
Because he is always for-getting.

●

What lives on its own body and dies when it devours itself?
A candle.

●

What is the age of excessive violence?
Outrage.

108

Scurrilous!

●

BILLY: What did you do when the ship sank in mid-ocean?
BRAG: Oh, I just grabbed a cake of soap and washed myself ashore.

●

What are diamonds?
Chunks of coal that kept on going.

●

What driver does not need a licence?
A screwdriver.

●

What is the height of foolishness?
Spending one's last dollar on a wallet.

●

Why do French farmers build their pigsties between their houses and their barns?
To make a home for their pigs.

●

JASCHA: When is a man wrecked on a desert island like a woman in a department store?
MASCHA: When he is looking for a sail.

●

SMART: Why do you call this the Fiddle Hotel?
SMARTER: Because it's such a vile inn.

110

POLITE CIVILIAN: How do you like life on the high seas?

BORED SAILOR: It's simply the knots!

•

What scales are not used for weighing?

The scales you practise on the piano.

•

Why did the jelly roll?

Because it saw the apple turnover.

•

Which is better: "The house burned *down*," or "The house burned *up?*"

Neither; they are both very bad.

•

Why is a bride unlucky on her wedding day?

Because she does not marry the best man.

•

TEACHER: What are the Phoenicians noted for?

STUDENT: Blinds.

•

Why is it vulgar to play and sing by yourself?

Because it is solo.

•

What is the best name for the wife of a civil engineer?

Bridget.

•

What age is a proverb?

Adage.

•

Why is a tin can tied to a dog's tail like death?

Because it's something bound to occur.

•

What is a shooting cat?

A catapult.

•

PAL: How did you get on at the police court today?
SAD SAM: Fine.

•

What fruit grows on telephone poles?

Electric currents.

•

Why does summer go so quickly?

Because there is often an evening mist.

•

What possible use was the eclipse?

It gave the sun time for reflection.

•

When is a little girl like an orange?

When she looks round.

112

●

Which flower tells what the dressmaker did when she sat on a pin?

Rose.

●

Where is medicine mentioned in the Bible?

Where the Lord gave Moses two tablets.

●

What dance is something to eat?

Abundance.

•

What is the largest vegetable?

A policeman's beat.

•

On which of Captain Cook's three voyages around the world was he killed?

The last one.

•

What is all over the house?

The roof.

•

Why is an extravagant person's purse like a thunder-cloud?

Because it is continually lightning.

•

What age is a platform?

Stage.

tortuous!

●

WHAT AM I? RIDDLES AND VERSES

My first is in come, but not in go.
My second is in deep, but not in low.
My third is in fire, but not in flame.
My fourth is in love, but not in game.
My fifth is in meat, but not in stew.
My sixth is in one, but not in two.
My seventh is in try, but not in fail.
My eighth is in head, but not in tail.
My last is is snow, but not in rain.
My whole is a famous author of Spain.

C-E-R-V-A-N-T-E-S.

●

My first is in even, but not in odd.
My second is in sceptre, but not in rod.
My third is in long, but not in short.
My fourth is in hunt, but not in sport.
My last is in waist, but not in girth.
My whole is a close neighbour of the earth.

V-E-N-U-S.

115

●

My first is in take, but not in give.
My second is in die, and also in live.
My third is in go, but not in stop.
My fourth is in raise, but not in drop.
My last is in where, but not in who.
My whole is a beast you see at the zoo.

T-I-G-E-R.

116

Unscrupulous!

DUMB: Do people get fur from a skunk?
DORA: My goodness, yes!—as fur as possible!

•

Why did Noah catch so few fish while he was in the Ark?

Because he had only two worms.

•

CURT: I understand that Cynthia's new boyfriend takes her to mystery plays instead of dances.
BERT: Yes. They tell me they love each shudder.

•

What is a classified cat?

A category.

•

Why should one never complain about the price of a train ticket?

Because it is fare.

•

ENGLISH TEACHER: Jimmy, what's the meaning of "unaware?"
JIMMY: It's the last thing I take off at night.

•

Why did the moron stick his head in the oven?

Because he wanted a baked bean.

•

What is a garden bell?

A bellflower.

118

Who was the first electrician?
Noah. He made the Ark light on the mountain.

Why did the dressmaker want to avoid the crowd?
She was afraid she would be hemmed in.

Why does Santa Claus always go down the chimney?
Because it soots him.

SMART: If you should put three ducks into a crate, what would you have?
ALECK: Easy: a box of quackers.

●

Why should you never put a clock at the head of the stairs?

Because it might run down.

●

What is the best name for the wife of a dancing master?

Grace.

●

Why is reciprocated love like gout?

Because it is a joint affection.

●

SIMPLE: They caught the burglars who robbed the hotel last night.
SIMON: How?
SIMPLE: They jumped on the scales and gave themselves a weigh.

●

What age is the act of pulling a barge?

Towage.

●

What ability is a sure thing?

Inevitability.

●

Why is a cat like a transcontinental highway?

Because it's fur from one end to the other.

120

●

If your uncle's sister is not your aunt, what relation-
ship does she bear to you?

She is my mother.

●

What kin sleeps a lot?

A napkin.

●

When may a man properly be said to be immersed
in his business?

When he gives a swimming lesson.

●

Who gets the sack as soon as he starts to work?

The postman.

●

What cane makes you hurry faster?

A hurricane.

●

How could you refer to a tailor when you cannot
remember his name?

As Mr. Sew-and-Sew.

●

Where did the Thief of Baghdad live?

At Baghdad, of course.

•

JERRY: What makes your sister so fat lately—she used to be very thin?
TERRY: She's working in a photographer's shop.
JERRY: Why, how does that make any difference?
TERRY: Well, you see, she's in the developing room most of the time.

•

What age is teaching?
Tutelage.

•

How long will an eight-day clock run without winding?
It won't run at all without winding.

•

FRIEND: Do you plan to hunt lions again this season?
HUNTER: No, I'm going to look for gnu game.

•

What is the best system of book-keeping?
Never lend them.

•

What lice go to church?
Surplice.

•

What is an echo?
No sooner said than said.

122

●

If a man and a goose were in a runaway balloon and the man had no parachute, how could he get down?

He could pluck the goose.

●

What is a match?

Something that never strikes twice in any place.

●

What does a bride usually think as she walks into the church?

Aisle, Altar, Hymn.

●

What is the difference between an auction and sea-sickness?

One is a sale of effects, the other the effects of a sail.

●

What is a half-wit?

A person who spends half his time thinking up jokes and clever things to say.

●

Why is a cautious man like a pin?

Because his head prevents his going too far.

●

Why is a dog's tail a great novelty?

Because no-one ever saw it before.

●

SANDY: Well, all right then, if you won't lend me the money, I'll haunt you when I die!
ANDY: You can't.
SANDY: Why not?
ANDY: You haven't got a haunting licence.

●

What is the age of great fury?

Ravage.

●

How did the pig build a place to live?

It tied a knot in its tail and called it a pig's tie!

124

●

SMART: What did a mother sardine say to her baby sardine when they saw a submarine?
ALECK: "Don't be afraid; it's only a can of people."

●

What drink is appropriate for a prize fighter?
Punch.

●

Why can a man never give a small party?
Because he will be a host himself.

●

What is the best name for the wife of a gambler?
Betty.

●

Why is a pretty girl like an excellent mirror?
Because she is a good-looking lass.

●

What does an artist like to draw best?
His salary.

Vacuous!

●

What is the difference between a professional fighter and a lapdog?

One faces the licks, the other licks the face.

●

What is the age to stir up anger?

Enrage.

MINISTER: Do you take this woman for butter or for wurst?

GROOM: Oh, liver alone, I never sausage nerve.

•

Why is a lawn mower given this name?

Because when you think you've finished, you just look round and always see mower.

•

What kin do you fear?

Kindred.

•

ENGLISH GIRL, *very highhat*: Sir! I'd have you know that my father is an English peer.

AMERICAN BOY: Oh, thass all right. My old man is an American doc.

•

What ability is lasting?

Durability.

•

When is a goat nearly?
When it is all butt.

•

Why is E the most unlucky letter?
Because it is never in cash, always in debt, and never out of danger.

•

What can be right but never wrong?
An angle.

•

What is the similarity between soldiers and dentists?
They both have to drill.

•

When are clubs for young people absolutely necessary?
When kindness fails.

•

Why was Adam an impolite man?
Because ladies should have been first.

•

Why is tennis such a noisy game?
Because every player raises a racket.

•

What is the right material for an inventor to wear?
Patent leather.

●

What animals do most ladies keep in their bedrooms?
Mules.

●

What is the best name for the wife of a fisherman?
Nettie.

●

Why is a bright, pretty and relaxed young lady like a spoon in a cup of tea?
Because she is in-tea-resting.

●

What would tickle a fat man a great deal?
A fly on his nose.

●

Why is an actor evasive?
Because he tries to be everything but himself.

●

Why is our country like milk?
Because it's ours.

●

What is the most dangerous kind of assassin?
One who takes life easily.

●

What age is a likeness?
An image.

130

●

Why is a sculptor always an unhappy man?

Because he makes faces and busts.

●

What ability is a garment?

Suit-ability.

●

LEO: So you liked me because I paid no attention to you?

CLEO: Yes, it was love at first slight.

●

What dance is repeated?

Redundance.

•

Why does a dog bite his tail?
Easy—to make both ends meet.

•

What songs should only be sung by men?
Hymns.

•

What is a subterranean cat?
A catacomb.

Still more Etcetera!

●

VARIABLE VERBS

A boy who swims may say he swum,
But milk is skimmed and seldom skum,
And nails you trim, they are not trum.
When words you speak, these words are spoken,
But a nose is tweaked and can't be twoken,
And what you seek is seldom soken.
If we forget, then we've forgotten,
But things we wet are never wotten,
And houses let cannot be lotten.
The goods one sells are always sold
But fears dispelled are not dispold,
And what you smell is never smold.
When young, a top you oft saw spun,
But did you see a grin e'er grun,
Or a potato nearly skun?

There was a young lady who tried
A diet of apples, and died.
    The unfortunate miss
    Really perished of this:
Too much cider inside her inside.

THE PUN

"A pun is the lowest form of wit,"
It does not tax the brain a bit;
One merely takes a word that's plain
And picks one out that sounds the same.
Perhaps some letter may be changed
Or others slightly disarranged,
This to the meaning gives a twist,
Which much delights the humorist;
A sample now may help to show
The way a good pun ought to go:
"It isn't the cough that carries you off,
It's the coffin they carry you off in."

There was a young man so benighted,
He never knew when he was slighted;
    He would go to a party,
    And eat just as hearty,
As if he'd been really invited.

134

•

A diner while dining at Crewe
Found a rather large mouse in his stew.
  Said the waiter "Don't shout
  And wave it about,
Or the rest will be wanting one, too."

•

The Reverend Henry Ward Beecher
Called a hen a most elegant creature.
  The hen, pleased with that,
  Laid an egg in his hat,
And thus did the hen reward Beecher!

•

Into the coop the rooster rolls an ostrich egg;
  The hens he faces.
"Not to chide or deride, but only to show
What's being done in other places."

•

A new servant maid named Maria,
Had trouble in lighting the fire.
  The wood being green,
  She used gasoline . . .
Her position by now is much higher!

135

●

Jones has a lovely baby girl,
    The stork left her with a flutter;
Jones named her "Oleomargarine,"
    For he hadn't any but her.

●

'Twixt the optimist and the pessimist
    The difference is droll:
The optimist sees the doughnut
    While the pessimist sees the hole.

●

I envy you, lucky lightning bug,
You worry not a bit,
For when you see a traffic cop,
You know your tail-light's lit.

eXasperating!

•

How can you make a slow horse fast?

Tie him up.

•

If a girl falls into a well, why can her brother not help her?

Because he cannot be a brother and assist her too.

•

What happened when the moron got mixed up in the traffic jam?

A truck came along and gave him a big jar.

•

What is big enough to hold a pig, important enough to make quite a mark, yet small enough to hold in your hand?

A pen.

•

What people are terribly strong?

Shoplifters.

●

If a boy swallowed firecrackers, when would you
you know he was all right?

After hearing the last report.

●

What is the biggest jewel in the world?

A baseball diamond.

●

"Have you much fish in your basket?" asked a
neighbour one evening of a returning fisherman.
"Yes, a good eel," was the rather slippery reply.

•

What age is something attached?
Appendage.

•

Why is a crossword puzzle like a quarrel?
Because one word leads to another.

•

What huge body has five eyes, but cannot see?
The Mississippi River.

•

How do you change a local inhabitant?
Alternative.

•

Why would a compliment from a chicken be an insult?
Because it would be fowl language.

•

What is the age of resistance of an electrical conductor?
Ohmage.

•

TEACHER: What's a myth?
JOHNNY: A myth is a young female moth.

●

What is a fan?

A machine that hopes it can be an aircraft propeller when it grows up.

●

REX: When I was skiing in Switzerland, I slept in a bed twenty feet long and ten feet wide!
TEX: Sounds like a lot of bunk to me.

●

Why are cowards like butter?
They run before fire.

●

Where does the captain of a ship keep his poultry?
In the hatchway.

●

What special beverage is suitable for a chicken farmer?
A cocktail.

●

Why is a poor joke like a broken pencil?
Because it has no point.

●

ROBBY: Who was the smallest man in history?
BOBBY: The Roman soldier who went to sleep on his watch.

140

•

What are the neighbours of a saxophone player apt
to do that his fingers always do?
They move quickly.

•

What is a fool?
One who doesn't know anything, and doesn't know
that he doesn't know anything.

•

What age is a home for parentless children?
Orphanage.

•

What musical key cannot vote?
A-minor.

•

What did Juliet say to Romeo, when he moaned,
"Juliet, dearest, I'm burning with love for you?"
"Now, now, Romeo, don't make a fuel of yourself!"

JOLLY JIM: The roosters do the strutting while the hens do the laying. But that old hen wasn't doing anything so I'm gladiator.

•

When you listen to your little brother's drum, why are you like a just judge?
Because you hear both sides.

•

Why did Tony's wife make him give up his job as a travelling salesman?
She wanted her Tony home permanent.

•

What are assets?
Little donkeys.

•

What kind of birds should be kept behind bars?
Jail birds.

•

FASTIDIOUS: Shall I put chlorine in the water?
PUGNACIOUS: Sure—put her in if she needs a bath.

•

Why was the farmer driving along at ten miles an hour with that load of pigs?
He was looking for a porking place.

142

●

What is an autobiography?

A history of automobiles.

●

What is the age of bestowing favours?

Patronage.

●

Why did the fellow call his girl "Peach?"

Because she had a heart of stone.

●

What about the chap who stayed up all night figuring out where the sun went when it went down?

It finally dawned on him.

●

What does germinate mean?

To become a naturalized German.

●

Why do so many dentists get fat?

Nearly everything they touch is filling.

●

Why did the man refuse the package he received, where the name was obliterated?

Because his name was really Smith.

●

What's an eavesdropper?

An icicle.

•

Why is a single person like borrowed money?
Because he is alone.

•

What is it that the man who makes it does not need, the man who buys it does not use for himself, and the person who uses it does so without knowing it?
A coffin.

•

What is a circle?
A round straight line with a hole in the middle.

•

Why was the officer punished because he refused, at gun practice, the order to fire at will?
He didn't know which one Will was.

•

What kind of business never makes progress?
The stationery business.

•

DUMB DORA thinks the equator is a menagerie lion running around the earth.

•

What is a gold-digger?
A girl who likes to go buy-buy.

•

How can it be proved that a horse has six legs?
He has fore legs in front and two behind.

144

•

What is a good example of a collective noun?
A garbage can.

•

What is a fireplace?
An office used for discharging people.

•

If *some* people thirst after fame, some after knowledge, and some after money, what do they *all* thirst after?
Salted peanuts.

•

What is a dimple?
A bump inside out.

•

DOPEY DAN is so dumb that he thinks rhubarb is a French street.

•

Why was the new young student kicked out of school for cheating?
He was caught counting his ribs during the biology exam.

•

What age is the cost of hauling goods?
Truckage.

●

What is the best name for the wife of a jeweller?

Ruby.

●

What happened to the rider who wanted to go one way and the horse wanted to go the other way?

The horse tossed him for it.

●

ROCKY: What is untold wealth?
FELLER: That which does not appear on income tax reports.

●

What did the fellow plan to grow on the farm he bought—eight miles long and two inches wide?

Runner beans.

●

DOPEY DONNA bought three loaves of bread to economize, because she saw a sign in the baker's window that read:

Raisin bread tomorrow.

●

If she wants an escort—

Conductor.

146

RENDALL: *Why* is it easier to be a clergyman than a physician?
WENDALL: Ho! Anyone knows it's easier to preach than to practise.

If she's slow of comprehension—

Accelerator.

•

Why did the little city boy refuse to spend the summer on a farm in the country?

He heard they had thrashing machines there, and he didn't want to take a chance.

•

If the class has a head and the class has a foot, what's in between?

The student body.

•

Why did the young man nickname his girl friend "Appendix?"

Because it cost so much to take her out!

•

What is a college for crazy people?

A luniversity.

more and more etcetera!

●

THE BLIND MEN
AND THE ELEPHANT

It was six men of Indostan
   To learning much inclined,
Who went to see the elephant
   (Though all of them were blind),
That each by observation
   Might satisfy his mind.

The First approached the elephant,
   And, happening to fall
Against his broad and sturdy side,
   At once began to bawl:
"God bless me! but the elephant
   Is nothing but a wall!"

The Second, feeling of the tusk,
   Cried: "Ho! what have we here
So very round and smooth and sharp?
   To me 'tis mighty clear
This wonder of an elephant
   Is very like a spear!"

The Third approached the animal,
    And, happening to take
The squirming trunk within his hands,
    Thus boldly up and spake:
"I see," quoth he, "the elephant
    Is very like a snake!"

The Fourth reached out his eager hand,
    And felt about the knee:
"What most this wondrous beast is like
    Is mighty plain," quoth he;
" 'Tis clear enough the elephant
    Is very like a tree."

The Fifth, who chanced to touch the ear,
    Said: "E'en the blindest man
Can tell what this resembles most;
    Deny the fact who can,
This marvel of an elephant
    Is very like a fan!"

The Sixth no sooner had begun
    About the beast to grope,
Than, seizing on the swinging tail
    That fell within his scope,
"I see," quoth he, "the elephant
    Is very like a rope!"

And so these men of Indostan
   Disputed loud and long,
Each in his own opinion
   Exceeding stiff and strong,
Though each was partly in the right,
   And all were in the wrong!

So, oft in theologic wars
   The disputants, I ween,
Rail on in utter ignorance
   Of what each other mean,
And prate about an elephant
   Not one of them has seen!

                —*John Godfrey Saxe.*

●

An oyster from Timbuctoo
Confessed he was feeling quite blue,
   "For," he said, "as a rule,
   When the weather turns cool,
I invariably get into a stew!"

●

There was a kind curate of Kew,
Who kept a large cat in a pew;
   There he taught it each week
   A new letter of Greek,
But it never got further than *Mu.*

•

Epitaph on a Dentist
Stranger, approach this spot with gravity—
John Brown is filling his last cavity.

•

GETTING AHEAD

"What is the secret of success?" asked the Sphinx.

"Push," said the Button.

"Never be led," said the Pencil.

"Take pains," said the Window.

"Always keep cool," said the Ice.

"Be up to date," said the Calendar.

"Never lose your head," said the Barrel.

"Make light of everything," said the Fire.

"Do a driving business," said the Hammer.

"Aspire to greater things," said the Nutmeg.

"Be sharp in all your dealings," said the Knife.

"Find a good thing and stick to it," said the Glue.

Zealous!

●

What cap is never worn on the head?
A knee cap.

●

Why was the grocer chosen to play the bass drum in the band?
Because he is an honest fellow and gives full weight to every pound.

●

What are freckles?
Sun kisses.

●

With what would you fill a barrel to make it lighter than when it is empty?
Holes.

●

How are car sales recorded?
In an autograph.

•

What was the weather report from Mexico?

Chili today and hot tamale.

•

Why did the student call the hero of his story "Adam?"

The teacher told him to write it in the first person.

•

PETER: How did the farmer know he had the laziest rooster in the world on his farm?
PAUL: That rooster never crowed at sunrise. He just waited until some other rooster did, then nodded his head.

•

What did Cleopatra say when Mark Anthony asked if she was true to him?

Omar Khayyam.

•

What professional man usually works with a will?

A lawyer.

•

Why does a stork stand on one foot?

If he'd lift the other foot, he'd fall down.

•

Why did the man have a pinched look?

He was riding in the patrol car.

154

●

What is the principal part of a horse?
The mane part.

●

Why do they plan to fight the Battle of Bunker Hill over again.
It wasn't fought on the level.

●

What does a girl need to capture a man?
Hequipment.

●

TEACHER: Use these words in one sentence: bear, boys, bees.
PUPIL: Boys bees bare in the old swimming hole.

●

Why is a hot dog something really splendid?
A hot dog is the noblest of all dogs, because it feeds the hand that bites it.

●

If you think she's picking your pocket—
Dectector.

●

What age is tied together in a chain?
Linkage.

●

What is the difference between a deer fleeing from hunters and a midget witch?

One is a hunted stag and the other is a stunted hag.

●

SMART: What is the difference between a timid child and a shipwrecked sailor?

ALECK, *grinning*: One clings to his ma and the other to his spar.

●

What are the most enchanting, dreamy things ever built?

Air castles.